The feudal system

I'M A VILLEIN. MY LORD LETS ME LIVE ON HIS LAND. IN RETURN I WORK FOR HIM. I'M A SLAVE—THE LOWEST OF THE LOW

AND I'M EVEN LOWER THAN YOU

I'M A FREE PEASANT. I FARM THE LAND OWNED BY MY LORD. IN RETURN I PAY HIM RENT. I'M POOR AND MISERABLE

I'M POOR, MISERABLE *AND* OVERWORKED

I'M A KNIGHT. I GET MY LAND FROM THE KING. IN RETURN I FIGHT FOR HIM WHEN HE NEEDS ME. NOTHING BUT FIGHT, FIGHT, FIGHT.

AND WHO HAS TO LOOK AFTER THE LANDS WHILE HE'S AWAY? POOR ME!

I'M KING. I GET MY LAND FROM GOD. IN RETURN I SAY PRAYERS, BUILD CHURCHES AND FIGHT FOR HIM. BUT THERE'S ALWAYS SOMEONE AFTER MY THRONE

AND I'M ALWAYS TRYING TO GIVE HIM SONS TO CARRY ON THE ROYAL FAMILY. WHAT A LIFE

I'M GOD. I THOUGHT I'D MADE ALL THESE CHAPS EQUAL. MAYBE MY OTHER SERVANT WILL SORT THIS OUT FOR ME ...

I'M DEATH. THEY'RE ALL EQUAL AS FAR AS I'M CONCERNED. BUT A DOSE OF PLAGUE WILL DO THEM THE WORLD OF GOOD

Place stamp here

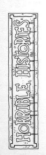

Guilds were groups of local craftsmen who performed plays for the people based on Bible stories. A lot of guild plays were rated PG — Pretty Gruesome!

Place stamp here

Middle Ages monks collected religious articles — like saints' bones — because they were said to have miraculous powers

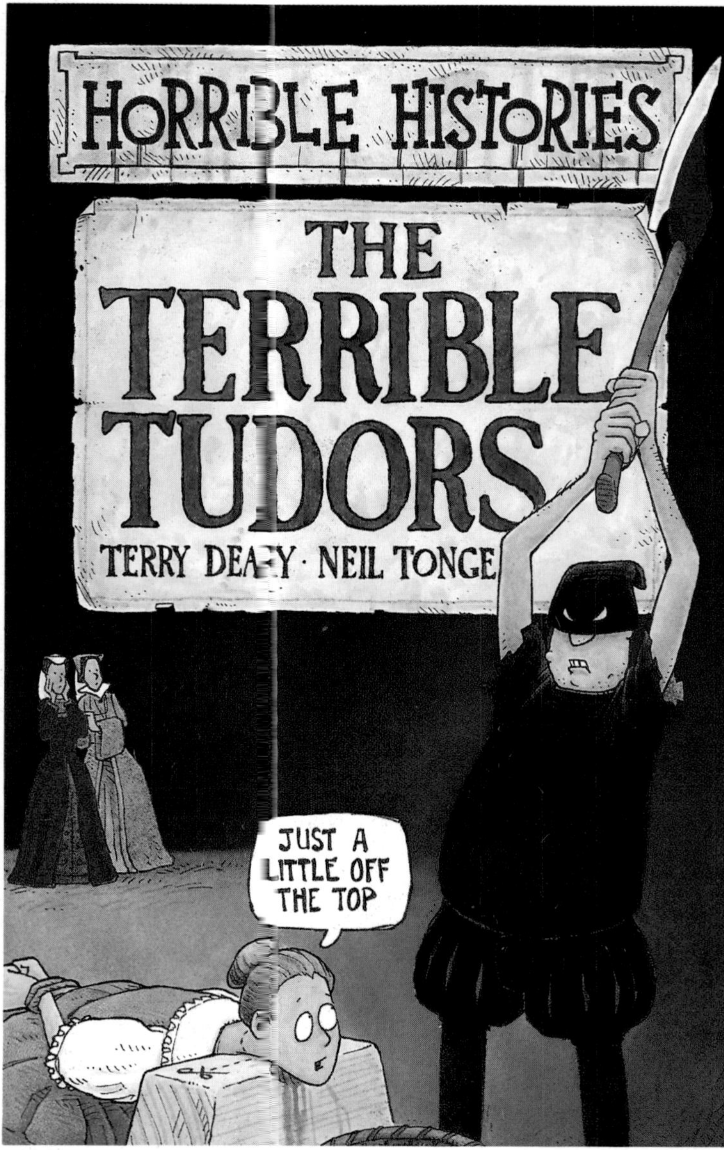
HORRIBLE HISTORIES
THE TERRIBLE TUDORS
TERRY DEARY · NEIL TONGE
JUST A LITTLE OFF THE TOP

Place stamp here

With open sewers and hole-in-the-ground toilets, Tudor streets were not renowned for their cleanliness.

Place stamp here

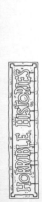

~ HENRY VIII's WIVES ~

GOOD WIFE GUIDE

—— CHILDREN ——	—— WHAT HAPPENED ——
⚲ GIRL ⚢ BOY	🦵 DIVORCED ✝ DIED
👒 NO CHILDREN	🪓 BEHEADED 👑 SURVIVED

CATHERINE OF ARAGON
QUEEN · Apr 1509 to Apr 1533

⚲ Mary I   🦵

ANNE BOLEYN
QUEEN · Jan 1533 to May 1536

⚲ Elizabeth I   🪓

JANE SEYMOUR
QUEEN · May 1536 to Oct 1537

⚢ Edward VI   ✝

ANNE OF CLEVES
QUEEN · Jan 1540 to July 1540

👒   🦵

CATHERINE HOWARD
QUEEN · July 1540 to Feb 1541

👒   🪓

CATHERINE PARR
QUEEN · July 1543 to Jan 1547

👒   👑

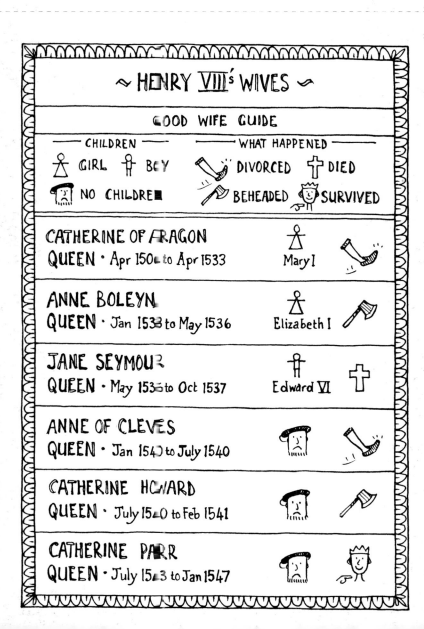

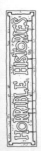

HORRIBLE HISTORIES

BANG!

The Stuarts invented a meat turner that used a dog in a wheel to roast meat over the kitchen fire.

Place stamp here

HORRIBLE HISTORIES

Guillotines were used in Stuart times. If the criminal had stolen an animal, sometimes the animal would be tied to the rope that released the guillotine blade, and driven away.

Place stamp here

BANG!

Place stamp here

Victorian Army officers lived like gentlemen and treated the men like servants.

Place stamp here

What the Sanitary Commission of 1855 found lurking in vile Victorian food.

Place stamp here

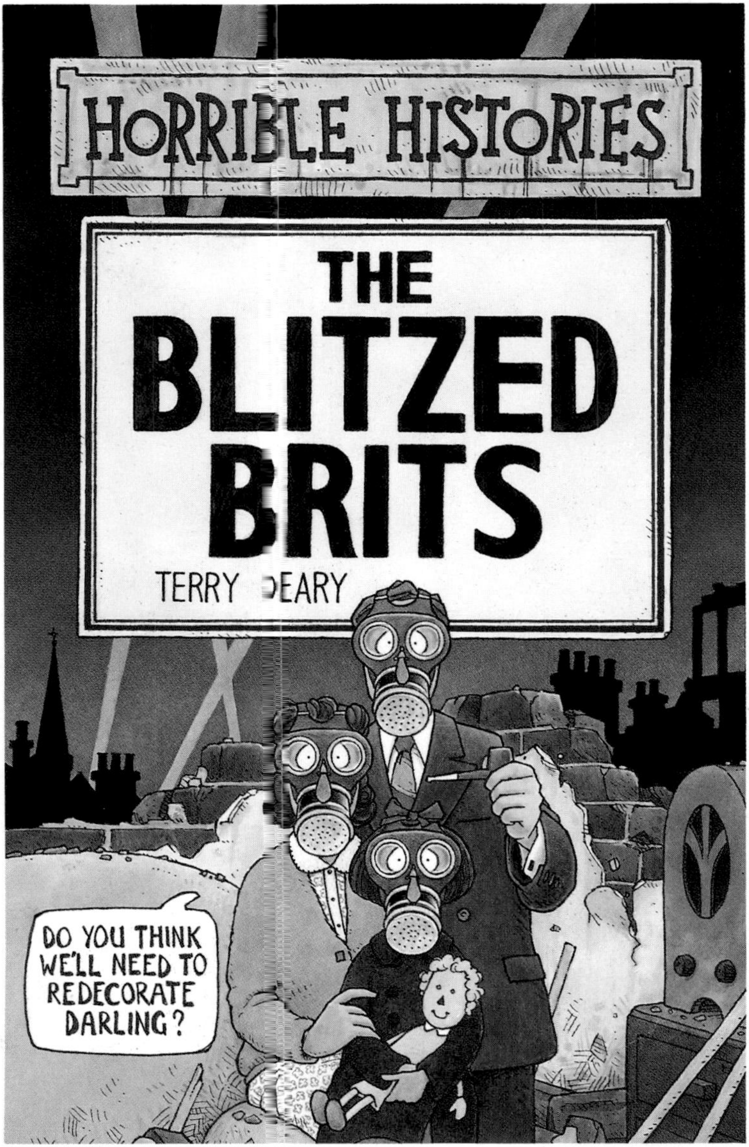
HORRIBLE HISTORIES
THE BLITZED BRITS
TERRY DEARY
DO YOU THINK WE'LL NEED TO REDECORATE DARLING?

When cities were bombed during the Blitz of the
Second World War, lots of people escaped from their
houses to the safety of their garden air raid shelters.
A popular style was the Anderson shelter.

Place stamp here

Petrol was rationed during the Second World War –
but luckily, household gas wasn't...

Place stamp here

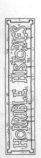